P9-DIA-196

The
SUPREME COURT

BY GEOFFREY M. HORN

WORLD ALMANAC® LIBRARY

Please visit our web site at: www.worldalmanaclibrary.com
For a free color catalog describing World Almanac® Library's list
of high-quality books and multimedia programs, call 1-800-848-2928 (USA)
or 1-800-387-3178 (Canada). World Almanac® Library's fax: (414) 332-3567.

Library of Congress Cataloging-in-Publication Data

Horn, Geoffrey M.
    The Supreme Court / by Geoffrey M. Horn.
        p. cm. — (World Almanac Library of American government)
    Includes bibliographical references and index.
    ISBN 0-8368-5459-4 (lib. bdg.)
    ISBN 0-8368-5464-0 (softcover)
    1. United States. Supreme Court—Juvenile literature. [1. United States. Supreme Court.] I. Title. II. Series.
KF8742.Z9H67   2003
347.73'26—dc21   2002038091

First published in 2003 by
World Almanac® Library
330 West Olive Street, Suite 100
Milwaukee, WI 53212 USA

Copyright © 2003 by World Almanac® Library.

Project editor: Alan Wachtel
Project manager: Jonny Brown
Cover design and layout: Melissa Valuch
Photo research: Brian Boerner
Indexer: Mary Brod
Production: Jessica L. Yanke

Photo credits: © AP/Wide World Photos: 4, 5, 6, 7 top, 12, 13 top, 15 both, 16, 17, 18, 19, 23 top, 29, 31, 34, 35, 36, 38, 39 both; © Brown Brothers: 30 bottom, 32 top; Collection of the Supreme Court of the United States: 11, 14, 20; © EyeWire: 37 bottom; © Hulton Archive/Getty: 30 top, 33 bottom; © IndexStock/Omni Photo Communications: 37 top; Courtesy Library of Congress: cover, 7 bottom, 8, 17, 25, 26, 27, 32 bottom, 33 top; Courtesy Maryland Commission on Artistic Property of the Maryland State Archives: 13 bottom; Courtesy National Archives and Records Administration: 23 bottom, 28; © Newmakers/Getty: 24 both; Courtesy The Ronald Reagan Presidential Library: 21; United States Department of Agriculture photo by Ken Hammond: 9; Melissa Valuch/© Gareth Stevens, Inc., 2003: 10

Printed in the United States of America

1 2 3 4 5 6 7 8 9 07 06 05 04 03

About The Author

GEOFFREY M. HORN is a freelance writer and editor with a lifelong interest in politics and the arts. He is the author of books for young people and adults and has contributed hundreds of articles to encyclopedias and other reference books, including *The World Almanac*. He lives in southwestern Virginia, in the foothills of the Blue Ridge Mountains, with his wife, five cats, and one rambunctious collie. He dedicates this book to the faculty and staff of Ferrum College.

TABLE OF CONTENTS

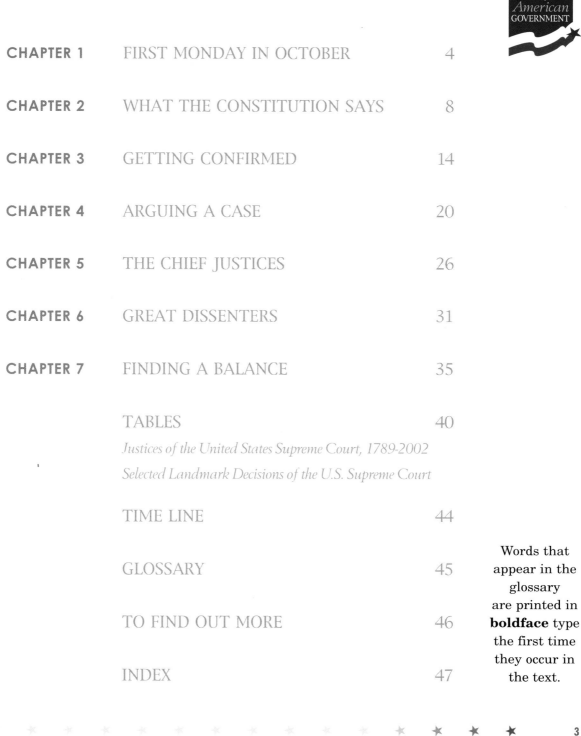

Words that appear in the glossary are printed in **boldface** type the first time they occur in the text.

FIRST MONDAY IN OCTOBER

For a lawyer arguing her case before the Supreme Court of the United States, there is something both terrifying and thrilling about this day. As the clock approaches 10 A.M., the session is almost ready to begin. White quill pens are laid out on the **attorneys**' tables, just as they were two hundred years ago. Reporters fill the red benches on the left side of the courtroom. They sit, notebooks in hand, waiting to hear the attorneys make their pleas.

The lawyer will have just half an hour to sum up her case, while the **justices** interrupt with sharp questions. One fumble, one stumble, and she could lose a case that has taken months or even years of preparation. Depending on the kind of case it is, her client could lose a fortune, maybe even his life.

Promptly at 10 o'clock, the marshal pounds his gavel. Everyone in the courtroom rises as the chief justice and the eight associate justices—all in black robes—approach their seats behind the raised mahogany bench at the front of the chamber. In a booming voice, the marshal calls out: "Oyez! Oyez! Oyez! All persons having business before the Honorable, the Supreme Court of the United States, are admonished to draw near and give their attention, for the Court is now sitting. God save the United States and this Honorable Court!"

▼ Spectators line up in front of the Supreme Court building on the first Monday in October, sharing the anticipation a new term brings.

THE SUPREME COURT IN AMERICAN LIFE

Each fall, as the Supreme Court holds its first session on the first Monday in October, many people wonder what the new term may bring. In a single term, which lasts until the end of June, the Court usually decides about eighty cases. Americans hold strong feelings about many of the matters that come before the Court: **abortion**, race relations, gay rights, the death penalty, flag burning, gun control, the role of religion in the public schools. People and groups throughout the United States look to the Court for guidance on these and other difficult issues.

The importance of the Supreme Court in modern times would have come as a great surprise to the **framers** who wrote the **Constitution**. After all, even though it stands at the top of the U.S. government's **judicial branch**, the Court has no power to raise and spend money, and no army to carry out its orders. One of the framers, Alexander Hamilton, wrote that the courts would "always be the least dangerous to the political rights of the Constitution," because they had "no influence over either the sword or the purse; no direction either of the strength or the wealth of the society." For more than one hundred and forty years, the Court did not even have its own building.

How did the Supreme Court win an equal place alongside the top offices of the government's **executive branch** and

▼ Abortion is one of the most difficult issues the Court has had to face in recent decades.

Landmark Cases—*Bush v. Gore*

More than 100 million Americans voted in the 2000 presidential election. But the outcome was decided by nine votes—the nine members of the Supreme Court.

In 2000, Texas Governor George W. Bush, a Republican, challenged Vice President Al Gore, a Democrat. The election was breathtakingly close. As the votes were counted, it became clear that whoever carried Florida would become the next president of the United States.

A first count in Florida showed Bush ahead by fewer than 2,000 votes out of some 6 million votes cast. A statewide recount by computer cut Bush's margin to a few hundred. Because the vote was still so close, Gore refused to give up. His lawyers went to court to demand that the ballots be recounted by hand in certain parts of the state. Bush's lawyers went to court to stop this from happening.

The legal battle continued for five weeks until the Supreme Court called a halt. No more recounts, the nine justices ruled, by a majority of five to four. In its unsigned opinion in *Bush v. Gore*, the Court said:

▲ The Court decided the election dispute between Vice President Al Gore (right) and George W. Bush (left).

> *None are more conscious of the vital limits on judicial authority than are the members of this Court, and none stand more in admiration of the Constitution's design to leave the selection of the President to the people. ... When contending parties invoke the process of the courts, however, it becomes our unsought responsibility to resolve the federal and constitutional issues the judicial system has been forced to confront.*

The landmark decision in December 2000 made Bush both the winner in Florida and president-elect of the United States.

legislative branch? One answer is that unlike the president and members of Congress—who must run for office every two, four, or six years—the justices of the Supreme Court may serve for as long as they wish. By making seats on the Supreme Court lifetime jobs, the framers hoped to protect the justices from the shifting winds of public opinion. More than any elected official, a justice of the Supreme Court is free to do what the law—and his or her own conscience—says is right. Also important is the doctrine of **judicial review**, the idea that the Supreme Court has the power to strike down laws that it judges to be **unconstitutional.** (See Chapter 2.)

▲ The decision in *Bush v. Gore* ended the recounting of presidential ballots in Florida.

▼ The Royal Exchange Building in New York City was the Court's first home.

A HOME OF ITS OWN

The Supreme Court met for the first time in February 1790, at the Royal Exchange Building in New York City. When the nation's capital moved to Philadelphia, the Supreme Court moved, too. During 1791, the justices met first in Independence Hall and

For most of the 1790s, the Court held its sessions in Philadelphia's Old City Hall.

then in the Old City Hall. During the next nine years, the Supreme Court shared City Hall with state and local courts, the Pennsylvania state legislature, and the United States Congress.

When the 1790s ended, the Supreme Court followed Congress to the new national capital in Washington, D.C. Congress, which had neglected to provide the Court with its own space in Washington, allowed the justices to begin meeting in 1801 in a small chamber of the Capitol. This was the building where the House of Representatives and the Senate also met. The Court moved to a different chamber in 1808, but this room proved so cold that, in February 1909, the justices held their sessions in a nearby tavern. Conditions got worse before they got better. In 1814, the British burned down much of the Capitol. While that building was being repaired, the Court held its sessions in a rented house.

After returning to the Capitol in 1817, the Supreme Court remained in cramped quarters for well over a century. The man who finally got the Court its own home in Washington, D.C., was William Howard Taft. Taft, who was president of the United States from 1909 to 1913 and chief justice from 1921 to 1930, is the only person ever to hold both jobs.

The cornerstone of the Supreme Court Building was laid by Chief Justice Charles Evans Hughes on October 13, 1932. Cass Gilbert was the architect who designed the building, which cost less than $10 million. About one-third of the money paid for the beautiful marble that decorates both its outside and inside walls. At the building's main entrance—the west front, facing the Capitol—are sixteen massive marble columns. Above them is engraved the motto "Equal Justice Under Law." The justices began their first session in their new quarters in 1935.

▼ **Constructed at a cost of less than $10 million, the Supreme Court Building is located in Washington, D.C., across the street from the Capitol.**

Chapter Two

WHAT THE CONSTITUTION SAYS

Article III, Section 1 of the Constitution places the "judicial Power of the United States" in the hands of the Supreme Court and lower federal courts. The same section gives Congress the power to create those federal courts below the Supreme Court level. Congress also decides which kinds of cases they may hear, how many judges will staff them, and how much these judges will be paid.

THE FEDERAL COURT SYSTEM

As set up by Congress, the federal court system looks like a ladder. At the ladder's base are the ninety-four judicial districts, each with its own district court. The district courts are where most federal trials are held. A large district may have two dozen judges or more, so many trials can go on at the same time. Also at the bottom of the ladder are certain special courts and agencies, such as military courts.

One level up from the district courts and special courts are the appellate courts, which hear **appeals** from decisions reached in the trial courts. These courts are grouped into twelve regions, or circuits. Each appellate court hears appeals from the trial courts in its own circuit. In addition, the Court of Appeals for the Federal Circuit hears appeals from the special courts and agencies.

THE UNITED STATES FEDERAL COURTS

SUPREME COURT	**UNITED STATES SUPREME COURT**
APPELLATE COURTS	**U.S. Courts of Appeals** 12 Regional Circuit Courts of Appeals 1 U.S. Court of Appeals for the Federal Circuit
TRIAL COURTS	**U.S. District Courts** 94 judicial districts U.S. Bankruptcy Courts **U.S. Court of International Trade** **U.S. Court of Federal Claims**
FEDERAL COURTS AND OTHER ENTITIES OUTSIDE THE JUDICIAL BRANCH	**Military Courts (Trial and Appellate)** **Court of Veterans Appeals** **U.S. Tax Court** **Federal administrative agencies and boards**

Counting the Numbers

One thing the Constitution does *not* say is how many justices should sit on the Supreme Court. Congress put the number at six in 1789 and has raised and lowered it several times since then. The number has remained nine—one chief justice and eight associate justices—since 1869.

In 1937, President Franklin D. Roosevelt tried to "pack" the Court by raising the number of justices to fifteen and filling the new positions with justices who agreed with his views. He was frustrated and angry because the nine justices then on the bench had ruled against many of his programs. Congress rejected Roosevelt's plan, handing him a severe political setback.

At the top of the ladder is the United States Supreme Court. Each year it hears cases that have not been resolved to the satisfaction of the losing side in the lower courts. Some of these are appeals from federal courts. Others are appeals from state courts. Each state has its own court system and even its own supreme court, but the United States Supreme Court is above them all.

In every case it chooses to accept, the Supreme Court is the "court of last resort." This means the Supreme Court has the final say. No further appeals are allowed.

▼ **The courtroom of the Supreme Court Building in Washington, D.C. Notice the nine large chairs at the front of the room, where the nine Supreme Court justices sit.**

SERVING ON THE SUPREME COURT

According to Article II, Section 2, the president has the power to select justices of the Supreme Court. The Senate then has the duty to review the president's choices and to accept or reject them by majority vote.

The Constitution says how old someone must be in order to serve as president or in Congress. Surprisingly, it does not say how old someone must be in order to

serve on the Supreme Court. The youngest Supreme Court justice in history was Joseph Story, who was only thirty-two years of age when he was appointed to the Court in 1811. The youngest justice now serving on the Court is Clarence Thomas, who was forty-three years old when he was approved by the Senate in 1991. As of 2002, Thomas was also the present Court's only African-American justice.

Article III, Section 1 provides for members of the Supreme Court to receive a salary. As of 2002, the chief justice was paid $192,600 a year, and each associate justice received $184,400.

Supreme Court "Firsts"

Most Supreme Court justices have been white, Protestant men. The first female Supreme Court justice was Sandra Day O'Connor, who joined the Court in 1981. The first black American to become a Supreme Court justice was Thurgood Marshall in 1967. When Marshall retired in 1991, his seat was the one to which Clarence Thomas was appointed.

Roger B. Taney was the first Roman Catholic to join the Court; he was chief justice for twenty-eight years, from 1836 to 1864. Louis D. Brandeis, the first Jewish justice, served on the Court from 1916 to 1939.

This 1991 photo shows the Supreme Court's first woman justice, Sandra Day O'Connor, seated next to Clarence Thomas, the second African American to join the Court.

"DURING GOOD BEHAVIOUR"

Unlike the president and members of Congress, justices of the Supreme Court do not run for reelection. Once confirmed by the Senate, they can—and often do—serve a very long time. The longest-serving justice in history was William O. Douglas, who sat on the Court for thirty-six years, from 1939 to 1975. Justice Oliver Wendell Holmes was approaching his ninety-first birthday when he stepped down from the Court in 1932.

The Constitution says that Supreme Court justices and other federal judges "shall hold their offices during good Behaviour." The only way to force a justice to leave the Court is through **impeachment**. Only one Supreme Court justice has ever been impeached: Samuel Chase, who served from 1796 to 1811. His case says a great deal about the relationship between the Court and Congress.

Chase held strong political views and was not bashful about expressing them. In the presidential election of 1800, he openly supported John Adams against Thomas Jefferson. Supporters of Jefferson, who won the election, thought Chase was biased. They said Chase's views—and the way he expressed them—were so extreme that he was not fit to remain on the Court.

Chase was impeached by the House in March 1804. The following February his case came up for trial in the Senate. His defenders argued that impeachment should only apply to high officials who had actually broken the law. Chase may have acted unwisely, they said, but he had not committed a crime. When the question came to a vote, the Senate cleared Chase of all the charges against him.

Two important lessons have been drawn from this case. The first lesson is that Congress should not try

▲ Congress passed and President Bill Clinton signed a law expanding his veto powers, but the Supreme Court, using its right of judicial review, declared the law unconstitutional.

▼ Associate Justice Samuel Chase was impeached by the House but cleared by the Senate.

to remove a Supreme Court justice just because members of the House and Senate happen to disagree with his political or legal views. The second lesson is that Supreme Court justices should avoid making specific comments for or against particular political causes or candidates. The Court, according to this view, should be "above politics."

Landmark Cases— *Marbury v. Madison*

△ **William Marbury's lawsuit became a landmark Supreme Court case.**

Marbury v. Madison (1803) was the case that, more than any other, allowed the Supreme Court to emerge from the shadow of Congress. The case established the idea of judicial review—the rule that the Supreme Court has the power to overturn any law that violates the Constitution.

Like the Chase impeachment, the *Marbury* case grew out of a dispute between the followers of Jefferson and the followers of Adams. Shortly before his term ended in 1801, Adams named a large number of judges. Most of them received formal letters signed by Adams telling them of their new jobs. By mistake, however, four men did not get their official letters in time. One of these four was William Marbury.

When Jefferson became president, his secretary of state, James Madison, refused to give Marbury the letter that would make him a judge. Marbury **sued**, asking the Supreme Court to issue an order that would force Madison to do what Marbury wanted. Congress had allowed the Court to issue this kind of order when it passed the Judiciary Act of 1789.

The Court faced two major questions. The first question was: Did Marbury have a right to the job? To this question the Court said yes, because Adams had signed the letter in time, even though Marbury had not received it. The second question was more difficult: Did the Court have the power to issue the order that Marbury asked for?

The answer to this second question is what makes the *Marbury* case so important. Writing for the Court, Chief Justice John Marshall said no. He argued that the Constitution was more important than any ordinary law. Because parts of the Judiciary Act were in conflict with the Constitution, those parts had to be struck down.

Finally, he wrote, "It is emphatically the province and duty of the Judicial Department to say what the law is." With these famous words he laid down the rule that the Supreme Court—and not the president or the Congress—would have the last word on whether a law is valid or not.

Chapter Three

GETTING CONFIRMED

Selecting a Supreme Court nominee is one of the hardest decisions a president can make. Typically, a Supreme Court justice will still be on the bench many years after the president has left office. A president who is concerned about his own place in history will want to choose a nominee who is well suited for the job. The president will also want to choose a justice who shares many of his own views on politics, society, and the law.

The choice of a Supreme Court nominee has become much tougher in recent decades. Because the Court deals with some of the most difficult issues in American life, the choice of a nominee can spark intense debate. Powerful interest groups will want to support a nominee who thinks their way on a particular issue—school prayer, for example. Other powerful interest groups with opposing views may do all they can to defeat that same nominee in the Senate.

⚖ **Ruth Bader Ginsburg (above, right) was known as a champion of women's rights when President Bill Clinton chose her for the Supreme Court in 1993.**

⚐ **Ginsburg wrote the important 1996 decision that required Virginia Military Institute to admit women as cadets (left).**

CHOOSING A NOMINEE

A president must consider many questions when choosing a nominee. First of all, is the candidate qualified? Although the Constitution does not require this, recent presidents have chosen Supreme Court nominees who were already federal judges. Nominees for the Supreme Court are rated by the American Bar Association (ABA), a national lawyers' group. If some members of the ABA rating committee call a nominee "not qualified," that may raise public doubts about the candidate's fitness for the job.

Second, will the nominee be able to win a majority in the Senate? If the White House and the Senate are both controlled by the same party, approval will usually be quick and easy. If, however, the White House and the Senate are controlled by different parties, the president must be careful to choose someone acceptable to party leaders on both sides.

Third, has the nominee done anything that might embarrass the president or the Court? In 1987, for example, President Ronald Reagan chose a federal judge, Douglas Ginsburg, to fill a vacancy on the Supreme Court. The nomination was dropped after the press reported—and Ginsburg admitted—that he had broken the law by smoking marijuana while he was a teacher at Harvard Law School.

▼ When this photo was taken in 1971, the Court had its first black member—Thurgood Marshall (back row, left)—but still had no women.

Fourth, how will the nominee affect the diversity of the bench? President Lyndon Johnson certainly knew he was striking a blow against racism in 1967 when he named Thurgood Marshall as the first African-American Supreme Court justice. Similarly, when Ronald Reagan chose Sandra Day O'Connor in 1981, he knew he was making history by naming the first woman to the Court.

▲ Before he became a Supreme Court justice, Thurgood Marshall (center) had a vital role in one of the most important cases ever to reach the Court: *Brown v. Board of Education* (1954), which outlawed racial segregation in the public schools.

Today, almost everyone agrees that the Supreme Court needs to include people of different backgrounds.

SENATE HEARINGS

When a Supreme Court justice dies or retires, the president sends the name of a replacement to the Senate, which refers the matter to the Senate Judiciary Committee. The nominee will then meet privately with senators on the committee, while the press, various interest groups, and committee staff members check out the candidate's life and career.

Normally after a period of four to six weeks, the Judiciary Committee holds public hearings. At these hearings, which are nationally televised, witnesses make statements for or against the nominee. The senators also question the nominee at length. The candidate will usually be willing to discuss legal matters in general terms but will refuse to discuss details of any case that might come before the Court.

Sometimes the questions focus on personal issues. In 1991,

▲ **Anita Hill complained about Clarence Thomas's behavior toward her, but the Senate confirmed him anyway.**

for example, the senators asked Clarence Thomas about a serious complaint by another black lawyer, Anita Hill. Hill, who worked with Thomas in the early 1980s, said he had sexually harassed her. Thomas angrily denied the charge, and the Senate confirmed him by a vote of 52–48. Even though he was confirmed, one senator who voted for him, Nancy Landon Kassebaum, a Kansas Republican, said Thomas would "live under a cloud of suspicion he can never fully escape."

WHEN THE SENATE SAYS NO

After it holds hearings, the Judiciary Committee votes on the candidate. If a majority of the committee approves, the nomination is sent to the floor of the Senate. Then, after several days of debate, the whole Senate either confirms or rejects the president's choice. Between 1789 and 1994, presidents nominated a total of 148 Supreme Court justices. Of these, the Senate approved 120— about four out of five. A total of twenty-eight nominees failed to make it onto the Court.

One of the most bruising battles came in 1987, when President Reagan named Robert Bork to the Supreme Court to replace Associate Justice Lewis F. Powell, Jr., who had retired in June. Bork, a well-known judge and legal thinker, held very **conservative** views on issues such as women's rights. If Powell had stepped down a year earlier—when Republicans controlled the Senate—Bork might have gotten a seat on the Court. But Democrats had won back the Senate in November 1986. They did not give Bork a very warm welcome.

The Judiciary Committee, after long and difficult hearings, voted against the nominee by a margin of nine to five. At that point, most candidates would have withdrawn. Bork, however, refused to step aside. Instead, he insisted on a vote by the full Senate. In the end, fifty-eight senators (including six Republicans) voted against him, and only forty-two voted in favor. Bork's supporters were bitter. They claimed he lost only because liberals disagreed with his political views.

⬆ **Former President Gerald Ford (left) spoke in favor of Robert Bork (right) in 1987. The Senate turned Bork down in a vote that angered his conservative supporters.**

Landmark Cases—*Griswold v. Connecticut*

In *Griswold v. Connecticut* (1965), the Supreme Court held that people had a basic "right to privacy." The Court said this right to privacy could be found in the Constitution, even though the word "privacy" does not appear there. At his committee hearings, Robert Bork made no effort to hide his belief that the *Griswold* case had been wrongly decided.

Griswold was a director of Planned Parenthood of Connecticut. As part of his job, he gave information about birth control to married couples. This broke a Connecticut state law, which said that anyone providing such advice could be fined, jailed, or both.

The Court found that the Connecticut law violated the Constitution by making rules about the private behavior of married couples. Writing for the majority, Justice Douglas argued that each specific right mentioned in the Constitution is surrounded by other rights. These rights, including the right to privacy, are real, even if it they are not specifically stated. Later court decisions have relied on *Griswold* in broadening the right of privacy to include behavior by unmarried people.

Chapter Four

ARGUING A CASE

E ach year the Supreme Court is asked to review more than 7,000 cases. Each proper request received by the Court is given a number and placed on a long list called a docket. The Court does not have the time to review every case on the docket. In fact, each year it can give a full review to no more than one hundred cases. The justices only write formal opinions for about eighty cases a year.

HOW THE COURT CHOOSES A CASE

How does the Court decide which cases to hear? At least four justices must believe the legal questions posed by the case are so important that they merit the Court's attention. The rules of the Court give several reasons why the justices may choose to take a case:

• A state supreme court or federal appeals court has "decided an important question of federal law that has not been, but should be, settled" by the Court.

▼ This is the conference room where Supreme Court cases are decided. The nine justices are the only ones allowed in the room when the decision is made; no observers of any kind are present.

- Lower courts have decided a question of federal law in a way that conflicts with previous Supreme Court rulings.
- An important point of law has been decided in conflicting ways by different federal and state courts.
- A state or federal court has acted in a way that seriously violates "the accepted and usual course of judicial proceedings."

WRITTEN AND ORAL ARGUMENTS

The Court receives written arguments and **oral arguments** for every case it chooses to hear. The written arguments are called briefs. Just because these papers are called "briefs" does not mean they are short. In fact, the main briefs in a

Addressing the Court

When all the justices were men, it was considered proper to address a justice of the Supreme Court as "Mr." Oliver Wendell Holmes, for example, was called "Mr. Justice Holmes." Today, however, a lawyer speaking before the Court would say "Justice Scalia" or "Justice O'Connor" or "Your Honor." The title "Mr." is reserved for Chief Justice William H. Rehnquist, who is called "Mr. Chief Justice." This form of address would certainly change if a woman were named to the position.

⬛ Since Sandra Day O'Connor (right) joined the Court, the term "Mr. Justice" has been dropped.

case may be up to fifty pages long. Briefs must be submitted by the people or groups who are directly involved in the case. Briefs also may be offered by the federal government, state governments, or various other groups that have an interest in the outcome of the case.

After all the briefs have been filed, the Court hears oral arguments. With few exceptions, oral arguments for each case take no more than an hour. Lawyers for each side get only half an hour to make their case. (See Chapter 1.) Usually a lawyer cannot say more than a few sentences without being interrupted by questions from one or more justices. Among justices past and present, Antonin Scalia is known for asking some of the sharpest questions.

Unlike almost everything else the Court does and says, oral arguments are open to the public. In 1953, the Court began making audio tape recordings of oral arguments; since 1993, the public has been allowed to hear these tapes. Oral arguments before the Supreme Court have never been televised live—not even in the most important cases.

PRECEDENTS

Every legal argument, whether written or oral, will refer to earlier cases decided by the Supreme Court or by other courts. These earlier cases are called **precedents**. In their briefs, lawyers on both sides of a case will suggest precedents they want the justices to follow. The justices will then choose which precedents they think have most bearing on the case.

Precedents are important. They send a message that what was law yesterday and law today will still be law tomorrow. They also reassure the country that when the justices decide a case, they are following the law and not just following their own whims and opinions. However, no Court wants to be a slave to precedent. If enough justices feel that a precedent was wrongly decided, the Court may choose to overturn it.

Landmark Cases—
Brown v. Board of Education

In *Brown v. Board of Education* (1954), the Supreme Court ruled that public school systems that forced black and white children to go to separate schools were illegal. The Court spoke loudly and clearly in outlawing **segregation** in the public schools.

The Brown case took its name from Oliver Brown, a minister who lived in Topeka, Kansas. Brown's daughter Linda attended grade school in Topeka. He was one of a group of parents who sued the Topeka school board when it forced black children to go to all-black schools.

The Supreme Court had ruled in *Plessy v. Ferguson* (1896) that "separate but equal" treatment for whites and blacks was allowed by law. For many decades, in fact, the "separate but equal" doctrine was used to justify unfair treatment of blacks in many parts of the United States. In the *Brown* case, the Court admitted it had made a mistake when deciding *Plessy*. It overturned a precedent in order to right a terrible wrong.

⚏ Oliver Brown's daughter, Linda Brown Smith (above), stands in front of a school that refused to admit her when she was seven years old. The *Brown* decision was hailed by opponents of school segregation, like those shown in the photo below. ▼

THE COURT DECIDES

After oral arguments are over, the nine justices gather in a conference room. Before they begin their discussions, each justice shakes hands with the other eight. This tradition serves to remind the justices that, even when they disagree, they all should be working toward a common goal. When the justices decide a case, they are the only ones in the room. No **law clerks**, no secretaries, no reporters, no observers of any kind are present. On a Court with nine justices, it takes five votes to make a majority.

Theodore Olson (top) spoke for George W. Bush and Lawrence Tribe (above, center) spoke for Al Gore when the Court heard oral arguments on the case that decided the 2000 presidential election.

Law Clerks

Each justice is aided by several law clerks, who usually work at the Court for a year. These clerks are the top graduates of the nation's finest law schools.

Like the justices themselves, most of the clerks have been white males. In recent years, however, the justices have been doing a better job of seeking out and hiring talented women, African Americans, Latinos, and Asian Americans.

When the Court hands down a decision, it usually consists of several parts. First comes the opinion of the Court—the majority decision—which is written by one of the justices in the majority. If the chief justice agrees with the majority, he chooses which justice will write the majority opinion. If the chief justice sides with the minority, then the longest-serving justice on the majority side chooses who will write the opinion of the Court.

The first version of the opinion is written by one of the justice's law clerks. The justice then reads this version and makes changes. Copies of the opinion are sent to other justices who may support it, and these justices add their own changes. As a result, the majority opinion may be revised a dozen times. Compromises must be made so the opinion reflects the different viewpoints of the justices who make up the majority.

Next, in some cases, come the concurring opinions. These opinions are written by justices who agree with the outcome of the case but feel the need to express their own views on why they made their decisions.

Finally come the dissenting opinions, or dissents. (See Chapter 6.) These opinions are written by justices who disagree with the outcome of the case and with the legal reasoning behind it. A dissent has no legal power on its own. But a well-argued dissent can raise important ideas that, years later, might become part of a majority opinion.

Chapter Five

THE CHIEF JUSTICES

Sixteen people—all white, all men—have held the office of chief justice of the United States. Many were well known figures in American public life before they joined the Supreme Court. One of them, William Howard Taft, was president of the United States before he became chief justice. Six were cabinet members, one was a U.S. senator, and another was governor of one of the nation's largest states.

The most important job of the chief justice is to preside over the Court when it meets in public or private. The chief justice cannot tell any other member of the Court how to vote on a case. When siding with the majority, however, the chief justice can affect the outcome by choosing who writes the majority opinion. On really important cases, the chief justice will often write the majority opinions himself.

In addition to presiding over the Court, the chief justice has other duties: As the country's highest-ranking judicial officer, the chief justice helps run the federal court system. Every four years, on January 20, the chief justice gives the oath of office to a newly elected president. And if the president is impeached, the Constitution requires that the chief justice preside over the impeachment trial in the Senate.

▲ **William Howard Taft was the twenty-seventh president and, later, the tenth chief justice of the United States.**

JOHN MARSHALL

Most legal experts agree that John Marshall was the greatest chief justice in U.S. history. President John Adams, who appointed Marshall to the Court in 1801, later called him "my gift to the American people." In 1990, a poll of nearly

Most legal experts consider John Marshall the greatest chief justice in U.S. history.

five hundred legal experts ranked Marshall as the best Supreme Court justice ever.

Marshall was born in Virginia in 1755. He was trained as a lawyer, but he was also a man of action, and he served with General George Washington in the American Revolution, the war that freed the American colonies from England. Before joining the Supreme Court, he was elected to the Virginia House of Delegates, served briefly in the U.S. House of Representatives, and was Adams's secretary of state. He remained on the Court until his death in 1835. Marshall wrote the Court's landmark opinion in *Marbury v. Madison*. (See Chapter 2.) He also wrote another important decision, *McCulloch v. Maryland* (1819). The central question in *McCulloch* was whether Congress had a right to set up a national bank that competed with state banks. The state of Maryland said no, because the Constitution did not specifically give Congress that right. Marshall answered that the right to set up a national bank was an implied power—it followed from other powers the framers had given to Congress. Congress could use its implied powers, said Marshall, as long as it used them in ways that were consistent with what the framers had in mind:

> *Let the end be legitimate, let it be within the scope of the Constitution, and all means which are appropriate, which are plainly adapted to that end, which are not prohibited, but consist with the letter and spirit of the Constitution, are Constitutional.*

This ruling was important in two ways. It allowed Congress to pass new laws to meet the needs of a growing and changing nation. And it made clear to the states that when Congress acted properly, the states would have to give way to the federal government.

EARL WARREN

Most experts today rank Earl Warren among the most successful chief justices. In his own day, however, views of Warren were bitterly divided. He was born in Los Angeles, California, in 1891. He earned a reputation as a tough crime fighter, enforcing the law as prosecutor for Alameda County and then as attorney general of California.

On December 7, 1941, Japan attacked the U.S. Navy base at Pearl Harbor, Hawaii, plunging the United States into World War II. As attorney general, Warren supported an order that forced about 120,000 Japanese Americans living in California, Oregon, and Washington to leave their homes and move to internment camps. More than two-thirds of those interned were U.S. citizens who had never done anything disloyal to the United States. In 1988, the U.S. government apologized to Japanese Americans for the "grave injustice" it had done them. Each of the 60,000 internees still living was offered a $20,000 cash payment.

Warren, a Republican, was elected governor of California in 1942 and was reelected in 1946 and 1950. In 1953, he was named chief justice by Dwight Eisenhower, a Republican president. This was Eisenhower's way of repaying Warren, who had supported his campaign for president in 1952. Under Warren, the Court issued many liberal rulings that outraged the president's conservative backers. Eisenhower later called his choice of Warren "the most damnfool mistake I ever made."

The 1950s and 1960s brought enormous changes in American life, and the members of the Warren Court felt that the law had to change, too. Many Warren Court decisions broadened the rights of ordinary Americans. *Griswold v. Connecticut* (see Chapter 3) and *Brown v. Board of Education* (see Chapter 4) were both

▼ The Court made many landmark rulings while Earl Warren (right) was chief justice.

Landmark Cases—Bad Law

History has been unkind to some Supreme Court decisions. Most experts agree that one of the worst decisions ever made by the Court was *Scott v. Sandford* (1857), also known as the Dred Scott case. This decision held that, under the Constitution, black slaves were the property of their owners and could not be citizens of the United States. The ruling, by Chief Justice Roger B. Taney, also said that Congress had no power to stop slavery from spreading to the newly settled areas on the American frontier. Taney's fateful opinion helped bring about the **Civil War**.

Another disturbing decision was *Korematsu v. United States* (1944). In this case, the Court held that forcing Japanese Americans to move to **internment** camps was legal. In his dissent, Justice Frank Murphy said the internment of Japanese-Americans who had committed no crime was based on prejudice, half-truths, and misinformation.

▲ **Japanese Americans being taken to internment camps in 1942.**

decided while Warren was chief justice. Under Warren, the Court also helped reform American elections and supported the right of a free press to criticize public officials.

One landmark ruling by the Warren court that made some conservatives furious was *Miranda v. Arizona* (1966). In this case, the Court supported the rights of criminal suspects against possible abuses by the police. Today, because of *Miranda*, police are required to read a warning like this to anyone they arrest:

- *You have the right to remain silent.*
- *Anything you say can and will be used against you in a court of law.*
- *You have the right to speak to an attorney, and to have an attorney present during any questioning.*
- *If you cannot afford a lawyer, one will be provided for you at government expense.*

Police at first complained about *Miranda*, but it is now part of regular police practice. A challenge to *Miranda* was rejected by the Court in 2000 by a vote of seven to two.

WILLIAM REHNQUIST

William Rehnquist, the sixteenth chief justice of the United States, was born in Milwaukee, Wisconsin, in 1924. He served in the Air Force during World War II and then went to college and law school. After a year and a half at the Supreme Court as a law clerk for Justice Robert H. Jackson, he settled in Arizona, where he made his living as a lawyer.

In 1969, Rehnquist came back to Washington to work in the Justice Department. President Richard M. Nixon appointed him associate justice in 1971. Fifteen years later, he was named chief justice by President Ronald Reagan. Rehnquist, who is an expert on impeachment, presided over the Senate trial of President Bill Clinton in 1999.

Before he was appointed to the Supreme Court, Rehnquist was active in politics as a conservative Republican. On the bench, he soon became known as one of the Court's most conservative members. He opposed abortion, favored the death penalty, and moved to limit the rights of criminal suspects. Several far-reaching decisions by the Rehnquist Court upheld the rights of states against the growing power of Congress and the executive branch. Rehnquist also succeeded in winning support for his view that public money could be used to help fund religious schools.

On many issues, the Rehnquist Court and the Warren Court disagreed. But on one core question—the importance of judicial review—Rehnquist was fully in agreement with Marshall and Warren. Like those other two chief justices, Rehnquist has not been shy about using the power of the Court. He proved that when settling the 2000 presidential election in *Bush v. Gore.* (See Chapter 1.)

▼ While Senator Olympia Snowe (right) looks on, Senator Strom Thurmond (left) swears in Chief Justice William Rehnquist to preside over the impeachment trial of President Bill Clinton in 1999.

Chapter Six

GREAT DISSENTERS

▼ Because Hugo L. Black (below) was a member of the racist Ku Klux Klan (bottom) in the 1920s, critics doubted his fitness to serve as a justice. After he joined the Court in 1937, however, he became a champion of free speech and fair treatment for the poor.

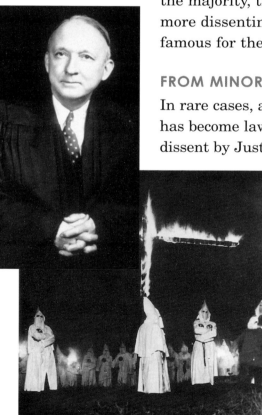

O n some important cases, the Supreme Court speaks with one clear voice. The Court was **unanimous** when it outlawed public school segregation in *Brown v. Board of Education*. The Court also spoke unanimously in *United States v. Nixon* (1974), when it ruled that the president of the United States could not withhold possible evidence of a crime.

In many Supreme Court cases, however, the decision is far from unanimous. For example, of the seventy-nine cases decided between October 2001 and June 2002, twenty-one were decided by the narrowest possible margin: five votes to four. When justices disagree with a decision reached by the majority, they often express their views in one or more dissenting opinions. Certain justices have become famous for the power and passion of their dissents.

FROM MINORITY TO MAJORITY

In rare cases, a view first expressed in a dissenting opinion has become law decades later. One example of this is the dissent by Justice Hugo L. Black in *Betts v. Brady* (1942). In *Betts*, the Court ruled that when a poor person was charged with a crime, a state court was usually not required to pay for a lawyer. In his dissent, Black pointed out how unfair this was: "A practice cannot be reconciled with 'common and fundamental ideas of fairness and right,' which subjects innocent men to increased dangers of conviction merely because of their poverty."

Black, who remained on the Supreme Court from 1937 to 1971, lived long enough to write the Court's unanimous opinion in *Gideon v. Wainwright* (1963). The *Gideon* decision overturned *Betts* and guaranteed a lawyer to everyone charged with a crime serious enough to be punished by imprisonment. The right to a lawyer is one of the "Miranda rights" that police must read to anyone they arrest. (See Chapter 5.)

Landmark Cases—
Morrison v. Olson

The Constitution makes the president the nation's chief law enforcement officer. What happens when a president or one of his highest aides is accused of breaking the law?

Congress tried to deal with this difficult problem in 1978 by passing the Ethics in Government Act. This law set up a new way of appointing an **independent counsel**—a special investigator or prosecutor. This prosecutor, who is chosen by a special court, cannot easily be pressured or fired by the president.

▲ Antonin Scalia is well known for his sharp questions and stinging dissents.

Opponents of the Ethics in Government Act said it violated the Constitution because it interfered with the powers of the president and the executive branch. In *Morrison v. Olson* (1988), the Supreme Court, led by Chief Justice Rehnquist, upheld the 1978 law. The lone dissenter was Antonin Scalia, who had joined the Court in 1986. In biting tones, he warned of the kinds of abuses that might happen when a special prosecutor was chosen by a panel of judges, as the law provided:

> What if they are politically partisan, as judges have been known to be, and select a prosecutor **antagonistic** to the administration, or even to the particular individual who has been selected for this special treatment? There is no remedy for that, not even a political one. Judges, after all, have life tenure, and appointing a sure-fire enthusiastic prosecutor could hardly be considered an impeachable offense. So if there is anything wrong with the selection, there is effectively no one to blame.

In time, some of Scalia's warnings came true, and the Ethics in Government Act was allowed to expire in 1999.

What's in a Name?

Known as the "Great Dissenter," John Marshall Harlan served on the Court from 1877 to 1911. He was named for John Marshall, who was still chief justice when Harlan was born in 1833. Harlan's grandson, also named John Marshall Harlan, was an associate justice from 1955 to 1971.

▶ **John Marshall Harlan, the "Great Dissenter."**

Another dissent that, decades later, became the majority view is the one written by Justice John Marshall Harlan in *Plessy v. Ferguson*. This was the 1896 case that said "separate but equal" treatment for blacks and whites was legal. Harlan's dissenting opinion has often been quoted:

> In view of the Constitution, in the eye of the law, there is in this country no superior, dominant, ruling class of citizens. . . . Our Constitution is color-blind, and neither knows nor tolerates classes among citizens.
> In respect of civil rights, all citizens are equal before the law. The humblest is the peer of the most powerful.

His attack on segregation was accepted by the whole Court in *Brown v. Board of Education* fifty-eight years later.

HOLMES AND BRANDEIS

▼ **Oliver Wendell Holmes, one of the Court's most admired members.**

Historians regard Oliver Wendell Holmes and Louis D. Brandeis as two of the greatest associate justices ever to sit on the Supreme Court. Born in 1841, Holmes was a member of the Court from 1902 to 1932. Brandeis, who was born in 1856, sat on the Court from 1916 to 1939. They served on the Court together for sixteen years and wrote memorable dissents in several landmark cases.

One of the most challenging cases they had to consider was *Olmstead v. United States* (1928). Roy Olmstead was a bootlegger—a person who sold liquor in violation of the law. Olmstead claimed that the government had tapped his phone line illegally. For that reason, he said, the evidence gathered by the government should not be used against him. By a vote of five to four, the Court held that using evidence from the wiretaps did not violate Olmstead's rights. Brandeis, Holmes, and two other justices disagreed, as did the Court in later rulings. In his dissent, Brandeis wrote these famous lines:

> *The makers of our Constitution. . . . sought to protect Americans in their beliefs, their thoughts, their emotions and their sensations. They conferred, as against the Government, the right to be let alone—the most comprehensive of rights, and the right most valued by civilized men.*

▲ **Justice Louis D. Brandeis joined with Justice Holmes in several memorable dissents.**

◀ **This 1922 photo shows police with liquor and equipment seized from bootleggers. Wiretaps used by the government to crack down on illegal liquor sales were challenged in the *Olmstead* case.**

"Fire!"

Probably the best-known words Justice Holmes ever wrote appeared in *Schenck v. United States* (1919). In *Schenck*, the Court tried to decide when the government could properly limit freedom of speech. Holmes argued that Congress had a right to restrict free speech when the words—and the time, place, and way they were said—posed "a clear and present danger." The Constitution, he concluded, "would not protect a man in falsely shouting fire in a theatre and causing a panic."

Chapter Seven

FINDING A BALANCE

No one can predict with confidence what the whole Court or any individual justice is going to do. Consider, for example, the question of whether a woman has a right to end her pregnancy by having an abortion. In his landmark opinion in *Roe v. Wade* (1973), Justice Harry A. Blackmun recognized two competing interests. The first was a woman's right to choose whether or not to have a baby, which the Court based on the right to privacy discussed in *Griswold*. (See Chapter 3.) The second was a state government's "important interests in safeguarding health, in maintaining medical standards, and in protecting potential life."

Blackmun tried to find a balance between the two. In the first three months of pregnancy, the Court said, the decision was strictly between the woman and her doctor. During the next three months of pregnancy, the state could regulate—but not ban—abortion to protect the woman's health. During the remaining weeks of pregnancy, when the baby was almost ready to be born, the state could outlaw abortion, except when having the baby might endanger the mother's life. The decision reflected the views of seven of the Court's nine members. One of the two dissenters was William Rehnquist, then an associate justice.

Two decades later, the Court was asked to revisit these questions in *Planned Parenthood v. Casey* (1992). By this time, Rehnquist was chief justice, and the Court had become much more conservative. Opponents of abortion hoped the tide had turned their way. Surprisingly, in

▼ Justice Harry A. Blackmun wrote the opinion in *Roe v. Wade* that made abortion legal in the United States.

Casey, a majority of the Court agreed with the main point of the *Roe* decision—that abortion was legal. Writing for the majority of the Court, Justices Sandra Day O'Connor, Anthony Kennedy, and David Souter chose to put aside their own views on whether abortion was right or wrong:

> *Men and women of good conscience can disagree, and we suppose some always shall disagree, about the profound moral and spiritual implications of terminating a pregnancy, even in its earliest stage. Some of us as individuals find abortion offensive to our most basic principles of morality, but that cannot control our decision. Our obligation is to define the liberty of all, not to mandate our own moral code.*

MORAL VALUES AND SOCIAL CHANGE

The abortion issue is not the only area in which the Supreme Court has had to confront deeply held beliefs. Another issue is gay rights. In *Bowers v. Hardwick* (1986),

▲ **High-tech security devices protect this Planned Parenthood office, which opened in 1998 in Boston, Massachusetts. Four years earlier, a gunman killed two female staff workers at abortion clinics in the Boston area.**

▲ Florida is one of the few states that still allows use of the electric chair to carry out the death penalty. Most states that have the death penalty now carry out executions by lethal injection.

the Court was asked to extend the right of privacy to homosexuals. In a five-to-four decision, the Court refused. Instead, it upheld a Georgia state law that made homosexual acts illegal. In another five-to-four ruling, the Court, in *Boy Scouts of America v. Dale* (2000), said that the Boy Scouts had a right to keep gays out. In *Dale*, both the majority and the minority noted that attitudes toward homosexuals were changing. For this reason, the Court will need to revisit gay rights questions in the coming years.

The death penalty is another moral issue on which opinions have changed. A majority of the present Court favors the death penalty in general. The justices take different views, however, as to when the death penalty may be fairly applied. In *Atkins v. Virginia* (2002), for example, the Court held that the state may not execute someone who is mentally retarded. In *Ring v. Arizona* (2002), the justices said the decision to impose the death penalty can only be made by a jury, not by a judge.

Because the Internet did not become popular until the 1990s, the law in this area is new. Should public libraries be required to censor or "filter" Internet sites?

▲ **Recent Supreme Court rulings have limited students' privacy rights.**

Landmark Cases— Students' Rights

When does a school's need to maintain order and discipline outweigh the rights of students as citizens under the Constitution? On this question, as on others, the balance of the Court has been shifting.

The liberal Warren Court upheld the right of students to wear a black armband as an antiwar protest. In *Tinker v. Des Moines Independent Community School District* (1969) the majority opinion said that students do not "shed their constitutional rights to freedom of speech or expression at the schoolhouse gate."

More recent rulings have given school officials greater leeway in restricting what students can say and do. In *Hazelwood School District v. Kuhlmeier* (1988), for example, the Court allowed schools to censor articles written by staff members of a school-sponsored student newspaper. In a series of decisions, including *Pottawatomie County v. Earls* (2002), the Court has expanded the power of school officials to test students for drug use.

Should certain kinds of materials sent over the Internet be illegal? Should you be able to copy and trade music

▼ **Should public libraries be required to "filter" Internet sites?**

and video files by top performers without paying for them? How private is your e-mail? The court system has just begun to deal with these and many other Internet-related questions.

FEDERAL AND STATE POWERS

In recent years, the Court has taken a new look at the balance between the powers of the federal government and the powers of the states. The Tenth **Amendment** to the Constitution grants to the states "or to the people" those powers it does not give to the federal government. For many decades, Congress expanded its powers, and the Court went along. During the 1990s, however, a majority of the Court, led by Chief Justice Rehnquist, began to say no.

A turning point was *United States v. Lopez* (1995), for which Rehnquist wrote the majority opinion. In 1990, Congress passed the Gun Free School Zones Act, which made it a federal crime for any unauthorized person to carry a gun near a school. Ruling in *Lopez* five years later, the majority did not deny that gun violence in and around schools was a serious problem. At that time, however, the Court struck down the law because it said that what happened in or near a local school was purely a local matter, and that Congress had no right to intrude.

⬆ **To strike a blow for states' rights, the Court struck down a gun-control law passed by Congress.**

FREEDOM AND SECURITY

Terrorists attacked the United States on September 11, 2001. Using hijacked aircraft, they destroyed the World Trade Center in New York City, damaged the Pentagon near Washington, D.C., and killed more than 3,000 people. Since then, Congress has passed laws giving the executive branch new powers to spy on, arrest, and hold people suspected of being terrorists. The U.S. government has claimed that it has the right to keep some suspected

terrorists in jail without spelling out the charges against them or allowing them to see a lawyer.

Does the threat of terrorism justify these limits on liberty? In time, the American people and the Supreme Court will give their answer. As Chief Justice Rehnquist has written:

> We cannot know for certain the sort of issues with which the Court will grapple in the third century of its existence. But there is no reason to doubt that it will continue as a vital and uniquely American . . . participant in the everlasting search of civilized society for the proper balance between liberty and authority, between the state and the individual.

⬛ The U.S. government's response to the destruction of the World Trade Center (top), the danger of bioterrorism (above), and other recent threats may require the Court to take a fresh look at the balance between liberty and security.

JUSTICES OF THE UNITED STATES SUPREME COURT, 1789–2002

(Chief justices are listed in blue)
(Current associate justices are listed in red)

Name	State[1]	Term	Years	Born	Died	Name	State[1]	Term	Years	Born	Died
John Jay	NY	1789-1795	5	1745	1829	Levi Woodbury	NH	1845-1851	5	1789	1851
John Rutledge	SC	1789-1791	1	1739	1800	Robert C. Grier	PA	1846-1870	23	1794	1870
William Cushing	MA	1789-1810	20	1732	1810	Benjamin R. Curtis	MA	1851-1857	6	1809	1874
James Wilson	PA	1789-1798	8	1742	1798	John A. Campbell	AL	1853-1861	8	1811	1889
John Blair	VA	1789-1796	6	1732	1800	Nathan Clifford	ME	1858-1881	23	1803	1881
James Iredell	NC	1790-1799	9	1751	1799	Noah H. Swayne	OH	1862-1881	18	1804	1884
Thomas Johnson	MD	1791-1793	1	1732	1819	Samuel F. Miller	IA	1862-1890	28	1816	1890
William Paterson	NJ	1793-1806	13	1745	1806	David Davis	IL	1862-1877	14	1815	1886
John Rutledge[2]	SC	1795	—	1739	1800	Stephen J. Field	CA	1863-1897	34	1816	1899
Samuel Chase	MD	1796-1811	15	1741	1811	Salmon P. Chase	OH	1864-1873	8	1808	1873
Oliver Ellsworth	CT	1796-1800	4	1745	1807	William Strong	PA	1870-1880	10	1808	1895
Bushrod Washington	VA	1798-1829	31	1762	1829	Joseph P. Bradley	NJ	1870-1892	21	1813	1892
Alfred Moore	NC	1799-1804	4	1755	1810	Ward Hunt	NY	1872-1882	9	1810	1886
John Marshall	VA	1801-1835	34	1755	1835	Morrison R. Waite	OH	1874-1888	14	1816	1888
William Johnson	SC	1804-1834	30	1771	1834	John M. Harlan	KY	1877-1911	34	1833	1911
Henry B. Livingston	NY	1806-1823	16	1757	1823	William B. Woods	GA	1880-1887	6	1824	1887
Thomas Todd	KY	1807-1826	18	1765	1826	Stanley Matthews	OH	1881-1889	7	1824	1889
Joseph Story	MA	1811-1845	33	1779	1845	Horace Gray	MA	1881-1902	20	1828	1902
Gabriel Duval	MD	1811-1835	22	1752	1844	Samuel Blatchford	NY	1882-1893	11	1820	1893
Smith Thompson	NY	1823-1843	20	1768	1843	Lucius Q.C. Lamar	MS	1888-1893	5	1825	1893
Robert Trimble	KY	1826-1828	2	1777	1828	Melville W. Fuller	IL	1888-1910	21	1833	1910
John McLean	OH	1829-1861	32	1785	1861	David J. Brewer	KS	1889-1910	20	1837	1910
Henry Baldwin	PA	1830-1844	14	1780	1844	Henry B. Brown	MI	1890-1906	15	1836	1913
James M. Wayne	GA	1835-1867	32	1790	1867	George Shiras, Jr.	PA	1892-1903	10	1832	1924
Roger B. Taney	MD	1836-1864	28	1777	1864	Howell E. Jackson	TN	1893-1895	2	1832	1895
Philip P. Barbour	VA	1836-1841	4	1783	1841	Edward D. White	LA	1894-1910	16	1845	1921
John Catron	TN	1837-1865	28	1786	1865	Rufus W. Peckham	NY	1895-1909	13	1838	1909
John McKinley	AL	1837-1852	15	1780	1852	Joseph McKenna	CA	1898-1925	26	1843	1926
Peter V. Daniel	VA	1841-1860	19	1784	1860	Oliver Wendell Holmes	MA	1902-1932	29	1841	1935
Samuel Nelson	NY	1845-1872	27	1792	1873	William R. Day	OH	1903-1922	19	1849	1923

Name	State[1]	Service Term	Years	Born	Died	Name	State[1]	Service Term	Years	Born	Died
William H. Moody	MA	1906-1910	3	1853	1917	Harold H. Burton	OH	1945-1958	13	1888	1964
Horace H. Lurton	TN	1909-1914	4	1844	1914	Fred M. Vinson	KY	1946-1953	7	1890	1953
Charles Evans Hughes	NY	1910-1916	5	1862	1948	Tom C. Clark	TX	1949-1967	18	1899	1977
Willis Van Devanter	WY	1910-1937	26	1859	1941	Sherman Minton	IN	1949-1956	7	1890	1965
Joseph R. Lamar	GA	1910-1916	5	1857	1916	Earl Warren	CA	1953-1969	16	1891	1974
Edward D. White	LA	1910-1921	10	1845	1921	John Marshall Harlan	NY	1955-1971	16	1899	1971
Mahlon Pitney	NJ	1912-1922	10	1858	1924	William J. Brennan, Jr.	NJ	1956-1990	33	1906	1997
James C. McReynolds	TN	1914-1941	26	1862	1946	Charles E. Whittaker	MO	1957-1962	5	1901	1973
Louis D. Brandeis	MA	1916-1939	22	1856	1941	Potter Stewart	OH	1958-1981	23	1915	1985
John H. Clarke	OH	1916-1922	5	1857	1945	Byron R. White	CO	1962-1993	31	1917	2002
William Howard Taft	CT	1921-1930	8	1857	1930	Arthur J. Goldberg	IL	1962-1965	3	1908	1990
George Sutherland	UT	1922-1938	15	1862	1942	Abe Fortas	TN	1965-1969	4	1910	1982
Pierce Butler	MN	1922-1939	16	1866	1939	Thurgood Marshall	NY	1967-1991	24	1908	1993
Edward T. Sanford	TN	1923-1930	7	1865	1930	Warren E. Burger	VA	1969-1986	17	1907	1995
Harlan F. Stone	NY	1925-1941	16	1872	1946	Harry A. Blackmun	MN	1970-1994	24	1908	1999
Charles Evans Hughes	NY	1930-1941	11	1862	1948	Lewis F. Powell, Jr.	VA	1971-1987	16	1907	1998
Owen J. Roberts	PA	1930-1945	15	1875	1955	William H. Rehnquist	AZ	1971-1986	15	1924-	
Benjamin N. Cardozo	NY	1932-1938	6	1870	1938	John Paul Stevens	IL	1975-		1920	
Hugo L. Black	AL	1937-1971	34	1886	1971	Sandra Day O'Connor	AZ	1981-		1930	
Stanley F. Reed	KY	1938-1957	19	1884	1980	William H. Rehnquist	AZ	1986-		1924	
Felix Frankfurter	MA	1939-1962	23	1882	1965	Antonin Scalia	VA	1986-		1936	
William O. Douglas	CT	1939-1975	36	1898	1980	Anthony M. Kennedy	CA	1988-		1936	
Frank Murphy	MI	1940-1949	9	1890	1949	David H. Souter	NH	1990-		1939	
Harlan F. Stone	NY	1941-1946	5	1872	1946	Clarence Thomas	VA	1991-		1948	
James F. Byrnes	SC	1941-1942	1	1879	1972	Ruth Bader Ginsburg	DC	1993-		1933	
Robert H. Jackson	NY	1941-1954	12	1892	1954	Stephen G. Breyer	MA	1994-		1938	
Wiley B. Rutledge	IA	1943-1949	6	1894	1949						

Justices are listed by order of appointment. Justices who are listed twice were first appointed as associate justice and then elevated to chief justice. (1) State of residence at time of appointment. (2) Named as acting chief justice; confirmation rejected by the Senate, Dec. 15, 1795.

SOURCE: *The World Almanac and Book of Facts 2002*

SELECTED LANDMARK DECISIONS OF THE U.S. SUPREME COURT

1803: *Marbury v. Madison.* The Court ruled that Congress exceeded its power in the Judiciary Act of 1789; the Court thus established its power to review acts of Congress and declare invalid those it found in conflict with the Constitution.

1819: *McCulloch v. Maryland.* The Court ruled that Congress had the authority to charter a national bank, under the Constitution's granting of the power to enact all laws "necessary and proper" to responsibilities of government.

1857: *Dred Scott v. Sanford.* The Court declared unconstitutional the already-repealed Missouri Compromise of 1820 because it deprived a person of his or her property—a slave—without due process of law. The Court also ruled that slaves were not citizens of any state nor of the U.S. (The latter part of the decision was overturned by ratification of the 14th Amendment in 1868.)

1896: *Plessy v. Ferguson.* The Court ruled that a state law requiring federal railroad trains to provide separate but equal facilities for black and white passengers neither infringed upon federal authority to regulate interstate commerce nor violated the 13th and 14th Amendments. (The "separate but equal" doctrine remained effective until the 1954 *Brown v. Board of Education* decision.)

1904: *Northern Securities Co. v. U.S.* The Court ruled that a holding company formed solely to eliminate competition between two railroad lines was a combination in restraint of trade, violating the federal antitrust act.

1908: *Muller v. Oregon.* The Court upheld a state law limiting the working hours of women. (Louis D. Brandeis, counseled for the state, cited evidence from social workers, physicians, and factory inspectors that the number of hours women worked affected their health and morals.)

1911: *Standard Oil Co. of New Jersey et al. v. U.S.* The Court ruled that the Standard Oil Trust must be dissolved because of irs unreasonable restraint of trade.

1919: *Schenck v. U.S.* The Court sustained the Espionage Act of 1917, maintaining that freedom of speech and press could be constrained if "the words used . . . create a clear and present danger . . ."

1925: *Gitlow v. New York.* The Court ruled that the First Amendment prohibition against government abridgement of the freedom of speech applied to the states as well as to the federal government. The decision was the first of a number of rulings holding that the 14th Amendment extended the guarantees of the Bill of Rights to state action.

1935: *Schechter Poultry Corp. v. U.S.* The Court ruled that Congress exceeded its authority to delegate legislative powers and to regulate interstate commerce when it enacted the National Industrial Recovery Act, which afforded the U.S. president too much discretionary power.

1951: *Dennis et al. v. U.S.* The Court upheld convictions under the Smith Act of 1940 for invoking Communist theory that advocated the forcible overthrow of the government. (In the 1957 *Yates v. U.S.* decision, the Court moderated this ruling by allowing such advocacy in the abstract, if not connected to action to achieve the goal.)

1954: *Brown v. Board of Education of Topeka.* The Court ruled that separate public schools for black and white students were inherently unequal, so that state-sanctioned segregation in public schools violated the equal protection guarantee of the 14th Amendment. And in *Bolling v. Sharpe* the Court ruled that the congressionally mandated segregated public school system in the District of Columbia violated the 5th Amendment's due process guarantee of personal liberty. (The *Brown* ruling also lead to abolition of state-sponsored segregation in other public facilities.)

1957: *Roth v. U.S., Alberts v. California.* The Court ruled obscene material was not protected by by First Amendment guarantees of freedom of speech and press, defining obscene as "utterly without redeeming social value" and appealing to "prurient interests" in the view of the average person. This definition was modified in later decisions, and the "average person" standard was replaced by the "local community" standards in *Miller v. California* (1973).

1961: *Mapp v. Ohio.* The Court ruled that evidence obtained in violation of the 4th Amendment guarantee against unreasonable search and seizure must be excluded form use at state as well as federal trials.

1962: *Engel v. Vitale.* The Court held that public school officials could not require pupils to recite a state-composed prayer, even if it was nondenominational and voluntary, because this would be an unconstitutional attempt to establish religion.

1962: *Baker v. Carr.* The Court held that the constitutional challenges to the unequal distribution of voters among legislative districts could be resolved by federal courts.

1963: *Gideon v. Wainwright.* The Court ruled that state and federal defendants who are charged with serious crimes must have access to an attorney, at state expense if necessary.

1964: *New York Times Co. v. Sullivan.* The Court ruled that the First Amendment protected the press from libel suits for defamatory reports about public officials unless an injured party could prove that a defamatory report was made out of malice or "reckless disregard" for the truth.

1965: *Griswold v. Conn.* The Court ruled that a state unconstitutionally interfered with personal privacy in the marriage relationship when it is prohibited anyone, including married couples, from using contraceptives.

1966: *Miranda v. Arizona.* The Court ruled that, under the guarantee of due process, suspects in its custody, before being questioned, must be informed that they have the right to remain silent, that anything they say may be used against them, and that they have the right to counsel.

1973: *Roe v. Wade, Doe v. Bolton.* The Court ruled that the fetus was not a "person" with constitutional rights and that a right to privacy inherent in the 14th Amendment's due process guarantee of personal liberty protected a woman's decision to have an abortion. During the first trimester of pregnancy, the Court maintained, the decision should be left solely to a woman and her physician. Some regulation of abortion procedures was allowed in the 2d trimester, and some restriction of abortion of the 3d.

1974: *U.S. v. Nixon.* The Court ruled that neither the separation of powers, nor the need to preserve the confidentiality of presidential communications could alone justify an absolute executive privilege of immunity from judicial demands for evidence to be used in a criminal trial.

1976: *Gregg v. Georgia, Profitt v. Fla., Jurek v. Texas.* The Court held that death, as a punishment for persons convicted of first degree murder, was not in and of itself cruel and unusual punishment in violation of the 8th Amendment. But the Court ruled that the sentencing judge and jury must consider the individual character of the offender and the circumstances of the particular crime.

1978: *Regents of Univ. of Calif. v. Bakke.* The Court ruled that a special admissions program for a state medical school, under which a set number of place were reserved for minorities, violated the 1964 Civil Rights Act, which forfeits excluding anyone because of race from a federally funded program. However, the Court ruled that race could be considered as one of a complex of factors.

1986: *Bowers v. Hardwick.* The Court refused to extend any constitutional rights of privacy to homosexual activity, upholding a Georgia law that in effect made such activity a crime. (Although the Georgia law made no distinction between heterosexual or homosexual sodomy, enforcement had been confined to homosexuals, the statute was invalidated by the state supreme court in 1998.) In *Romer v. Evans* (1996), the Court struck down a Colorado constitutional provision that barred legislation protecting homosexuals from discrimination.

1990: *Cruzan v. Missouri.* The Court ruled that a person had the right to refuse life-sustaining medical treatment. However, the Court also ruled that, before treatment could be withheld from a comatose patient, a state would require "clear and convincing evidence" that the patient would not have wanted to live. And in 2 1997 rulings, *Washington v. Glucksberg* and *Vacco v. Quill*, the Court ruled that states could ban doctor-assisted suicide.

1995: *Adarand Constructors v. Pelia.* The Court held that federal programs that classify people by race, unless "narrowly tailored" to accomplish a "compelling governmental interest," may deny individuals the right to equal protection.

1995: *U.S. Term Limits Inc. v. Thorton.* The Court ruled that neither states nor Congress could limit terms of members of Congress, since the Constitution reserves to the people the right to choose federal lawmakers.

1997: *Clinton v. Jones.* Rejecting an appeal by Pres. Clinton in a sexual harassment suit, the Court ruled that a sitting president did not have temporary immunity from a lawsuit for actions outside the realm of official duties.

1997: *Reno v. ACLU.* Citing the rights to free expression, the Court overturned a provision making it a crime to display or distribute "indecent" or "patently offensive" material on the Internet. In 1998, however, the Court ruled in *NEA v. Finley* that "general standards of decency" may be used as a criterion in federal arts funding.

1998: *Clinton v. City of New York.* The Court struck down the Line-Item Veto Act (1996), holding that it unconstitutionally gave the president "unilateral power to change the text of duly enacted statutes."

1998: *Faragher v. City of Boca Raton, Burlington Industries Inc. v. Ellerth.* The Court issued new guidelines for workplace sexual harassment suits, holding employers responsible for misconduct by supervisory employees. And in *Oncale v. Sundowner Offshore Services*, the Court ruled that the law against sexual harassment applies regardless of whether harasser and victim are the same sex.

1999: *Alden v. Maine, Florida Prepaid v. College Savings Bank, College Savings Bank v. Florida.* In a series of rulings, the Court applied the principle of "sovereign immunity" to shield states in large part from being sued under federal law.

2000: *Troxel v. Granville.* The justices found that a Washington state law allowing grandparents visitation rights, as broadly applied, interfered with parents' rights to determine the best care for their children.

2000: *Boy Scouts of America v. Dale.* The Court ruled that the Boy Scouts of America could dismiss a group leader after learning he was gay, holding that the rights to freedom of association outweighed a New Jersey anti-discrimination statute.

2000: *Stenberg v. Carhart.* The Court struck down a Nebraska law that banned so-called partial-birth abortion. It argued that the law could be interpreted as banning other abortion procedures and that it should have made exception for reasons of health. (See 1973: *Roe v. Wade.*)

2000: *Bush v. Gore.* The Court ruled that manual recounts of presidential ballots in the Nov. 2000 election couldn't proceed because inconsistent evaluation standards in different counties violated the equal protection clause. In effect, the ruling meant Bush would win the election.

SOURCE: The World Almanac and Book of Facts 2002

TIMELINE

1790	Supreme Court holds its first session at the Royal Exchange Building in New York City, February 1.
1791	The Court begins meeting in Philadelphia and remains there to 1800.
1801	John Marshall becomes chief justice. The Court meets for the first time in Washington, D.C., February 2.
1803	Decision in *Marbury v. Madison* establishes idea of judicial review.
1805	Senate refuses to remove Justice Samuel Chase from office.
1836	Roger B. Taney becomes first Roman Catholic to serve on the Court.
1857	In *Dred Scott* case, the Court says slavery is legal. The decision helps bring about the Civil War (1861–65), which ends slavery in the United States.
1896	Court upholds segregation ("separate but equal") in *Plessy v. Ferguson*.
1916	Louis D. Brandeis becomes the first Jewish associate justice.
1935	The Court holds its first session in its own building, October 7.
1937	Congress rejects plan by Franklin D. Roosevelt to "pack" the Court.
1944	In *Korematsu v. United States*, the Court upholds the internment of Japanese Americans during World War II.
1953	Earl Warren becomes chief justice.
1954	In *Brown v. Board of Education*, the Court reverses *Plessy* and outlaws segregation in public schools.
1967	Thurgood Marshall becomes first African American associate justice.
1973	Court legalizes abortion in *Roe v. Wade*.
1981	Sandra Day O'Connor becomes first female associate justice.
1986	William H. Rehnquist becomes chief justice.
1999	Rehnquist presides over impeachment trial of President Bill Clinton.
2000	Court decides presidential election in *Bush v. Gore*.

GLOSSARY

abortion: a medical procedure taken to end a pregnancy.

amendment: a change to the original Constitution; also, a change to a bill.

antagonistic: strongly opposed.

appeals: cases brought from lower courts to higher courts.

attorneys: another name for lawyers.

Civil War: a war (1861–65) between northern and southern states that began when the South rebelled against the Union. Slavery in the South was a major cause of the conflict, which was won by the North.

conservative: favoring traditional views and values, while seeking to slow the pace of social change.

Constitution: the basic document of the United States government.

executive branch: the part of the U.S. government headed by the president.

framers: a name for the group of political leaders who wrote the U.S. Constitution.

impeachment: the power of Congress to remove federal officials, including the president and Supreme Court justices.

independent counsel: a special prosecutor who investigates wrong-doing by the president or other high officials in the executive branch.

internment camps: places where the U.S. government confined many Japanese Americans during World War II.

judicial branch: the part of the U.S. government headed by the Supreme Court.

judicial review: the power of the Supreme Court to overturn any law that violates the Constitution.

justices: judges, specifically those on the Supreme Court.

law clerks: young lawyers who help the justices do their work.

legislative branch: the part of the U.S. government that makes laws.

oral arguments: one-hour sessions in which lawyers for both sides make their case, and the justices ask questions.

precedents: previous decisions that have some bearing on a current case.

segregation: separation of one racial group from another, enforced by law.

sued: brought legal action against; started a court case.

unanimous: without disagreement.

unconstitutional: not in agreement with the Constitution.

TO FIND OUT MORE

BOOKS

Compston, Christine L.
Earl Warren: Justice for All.
New York: Oxford University Press, 2002.

DeVillers, David.
Marbury v. Madison: Powers of the Supreme Court.
Berkeley Heights, N.J.: Enslow Publishers, 1998.

Fireside, Harvey, and Sarah Betsy Fuller.
Brown v. Board of Education: Equal Schooling for All.
Berkeley Heights, N.J.: Enslow Publishers, 1994.

Jost, Kenneth, ed.
The Supreme Court A to Z.
Washington, D.C.: Congressional Quarterly Inc., 1998 (2nd ed.).

Patrick, John J.
The Young Oxford Companion to the Supreme Court of the United States.
New York: Oxford University Press, 1994.

Rehnquist, William H.
The Supreme Court.
New York: Knopf, 2001 (rev. ed.).

INTERNET SITES

Appellate.net
http://www.appellate.net/sup_court/default.asp
Listen to oral arguments from about three dozen cases.

Cornell Law School, Legal Information Institute (LII)
http://supct.law.cornell.edu/supct/
Full text of current and historic Supreme Court decisions.

The Federal Judiciary
http://www.uscourts.gov/
Guide to the federal court system.

Oyez Oyez Oyez
http://oyez.nwu.edu/
Features a virtual tour of the Supreme Court building and a trivia game with a baseball theme.

Supreme Court Historical Society
http://www.supremecourthistory.org/
Detailed background on the history of the Court and its members.

Supreme Court of the United States
http://www.supremecourtus.gov/
The Court's official web site.

Index

INDEX

Page numbers in *italic* type refer to illustration captions.

INDEX (CONT.)